www.BeirBuaPress.com

The Nothingness Kit

by

John W. Sexton

Published by Beir Bua Press November 2022

ISBN: 978-1-914972-70-6

November 2022

Beir Bua Press, Co. Tipperary, Ireland.

Typesetting / Layout, Cover Design: Michelle Moloney King

Cover image: a visual poem by Michelle Moloney King

Ordering Information: For details, see www.BeirBuaPress.com

Published by Beir Bua Press - Printed in the UK

Our printer is certified as a B Corporation to measure our impact on the environment and help drive us to be even more conscious of our footprint.

9 781914 972706

The Nothingness Kit

John W. Sexton

For

Rich Magahiz

Friend, Poet
& Altered States Marshall

Muse-struck
the poets
loiter

Introduction

Transcending the Mortal Universe: Hybrid Gendai Scifaiku as Compressed Signal

Some years ago I began experimenting with scifaiku, a verse-form that was widely considered to be no more than a poetic ghetto. This supposed ghetto was disdained, vilified, shunned by many self-respecting haiku poets; and I entered it for that very reason. It was, in short, the perfect place for experimentation and development; potentially anything could be done with scifaiku because it was considered something of a verse rodent; a vermin glimpsed scurrying in the literary shadows. It was the perfect lab rat; very few loved it, cared for it or even cared about it. If poems die in the ghetto, nobody mourns them; if they are maimed, no one is particularly bothered. Here was a verse-form ripe for hybridisation, suitable for any mutations a poet might wish to impose. No one was overseeing any imposition of responsibility upon scifaiku, and responsibility is the enemy of literary experimentation; in the assumed ghetto of scifaiku I was free to be irresponsible; I was at liberty to be wild.

Scifaiku interests me because it has all the prophetic and satirical elements inherent in science fiction. It is also a perfect seed-bed for metaphor. As my minimalist influences I looked beyond traditional haiku: two important voices from the past were both from the Central and South Americas; one a poet and one a fictioneer. The poet was the Mexican metaphoricist haiku poet José Juan Tablada (1871-1945), and the fictioneer was the Guatemalan Augusto Monterroso (1921-2003).

Tablada was the first poet to introduce the haiku into Spanish poetry, but his own verse was fluid in the freedom of its imagery:

Pavo real, largo fulgor,   Peacock, long glare,
por el gallinero demócrata   you pass through the democratic
pasas como una Procesión ...   chicken-coop like a procession

Augusto Monterroso worked mainly in short fiction and was recognised for bringing innovation into the form; one of his more famous, and possibly notorious contributions, was his use of the single-sentence short story.

It was my idea with scifaiku to utilize Tablada's fluidity of image; to let metaphor infect everything. To my mind, the themes and subject matter of scifaiku should be all those elements common to the literature of science fantasy; from alternate history to alternate worlds, to future visions, to sociological satire, all of them encompassing the general impingement of the fantastic into the logical universe. It is also my contention that a single scifaiku should contain a discernible narrative or fantastic "situation". No less than its cousin, the fictional story, its scientific concept or premise should be encapsulated in a compressed "plot". The aim here should be to approximate what Augusto Monterroso was attempting in his celebrated minimalist fictions. Simultaneous to these aspirations, I was also heavily influenced by the more experimentalist approaches to haiku that are currently practised in Japan, most notably the gendai movements in contemporary haiku, as exemplified by haiku poets like Kôji Yasui, and such groups as the Chaos School.

Disdain from the mainstream notwithstanding, scifaiku is undoubtedly a rarefied Muse. In over a decade of hybrid gendai scifaiku composition the form has somewhat melded my poetic perception. Scifaiku is ultimately like a compressed message from another universe; is spastic through Space and Time. It is the voice of the oracle; the crossword puzzle clue of the Ouija Board. It does not need to be surrounded by white space as haiku usually demands; it is best left in the vicinity of chaos, vying closely with more of its kind, so that many scifaiku together can thus operate as a form of cryptic, seeping dream from the dense, garbled universe of the subconscious. Individual scifaiku move at velocity; they should thus be relentlessly hurled at the reader, one after the other in sequences like chemical code. Scifaiku is the Dark Matter of Poetry; penetrating everything, passing through all other Matter and Mind. It is the ultimate license for the poet, granting the liberty to be unstable.

Light

deep Martian aquifer -
a mollusc congress debates
the myth of stars

       drawn to chakra light...
       mothgods lapping nectar
       from the mind

through their smoky bodies
the starlight glitters -
meadow full of nothings

       Jack Russell barked open
       our sleep ... a halved snake
       leaks dawn

bubonic-skinned ...
all they knew of beauty
was themselves

       moist song of
       vulva birds
       sunlight through the gap

a grey dray-horse
its shadow dim ... the End
of Dull Days deadens

       badger moves the dark
       about in the dark ...
       night dense in the sett

oh you black sky ...
more visible
than the brightest stars

The Unwoods

telepathy ...
somewhere in the mind
an elephant

     albino badger
     transparent in daylight
     the unwoods begin

dandelion drift
Fukushima
leaks an heir

     anorexic girl
     stole a horse's shadow
     rode it into the ground

climbing down
on ladders of rain
the dead pass through us

     thrush ingmachines ...
     their earthworm accordions
     rend a soft tune

slit sea cucumber
bleeds dreams of light ... a knife
photographs the moon

     unscrewing re-screwing
     its head ... owl releases
     thought into night

is of star matter ...
no full stop before
or after infinity

A State of Mind

beneath their slant shoulders
zen spiral vortices ...
pines

> a bulb ruptures the city ...
> blossoms outdo the clouds
> scent engulfs us

Hansel's elevator of
goose down ... no thirteenth floor
no six six six

> fore! ...
> return of the prodigal golf balls
> all at once

Hildevarga's curse ...
dog-penis stinkhorns
stiffen by the convent gate

> unfolding the blueprint
> for fog ... everything
> is suddenly clear

the winged cows
milking them
is a state of mind

> pinpricks of rust
> the pontiff's tailor's pins
> all dulled with angels

sputum from
a seraphim ... galaxies fester
in his cough

Beaks of Nowl

I look up "parsec" ...
the turps scent of 60's
Asimov paperbacks

       let them eat cake
       Chef Frankenasty's
       evil marzipan creations

space is not black
starlight perforates
the prism spaceship

       ice crystals ...
       three-dimensional constructs
       of stop

moonstruck, the badger
lies dead ... his innards a ribbon
tying us down

       her pet malevolence …
       the witch strokes her fingers
       through the river sprite

interpreting the yews ...
on my palm
a woodlouse savant

       the dead eye
       of Polyphemus ... seconded sight
       has seen but does not see

multidimensional
beaks of nowl ... rip mice from
the allworlds at once

Electric Eel Radio

angels excreting space …
how else
did it get there?

> the soul impaled
> rides upon a porcupine
> into paradise

bright inside the whale
we send a distress …
electric eel radio

> silver shadows
> of Undone Town …
> the dark in shreds

the angel's zoot suit
had endless stripes
just endless

> inside father's watch
> coils of silverfish beat seconds
> of mortal time

translucent horns
rise from the asteroid …
slowly the lowly space snail

> grandroid puts 'em to sleep:
> one more Jack Hammer
> and Brer Rivet story

Rachel goes down
… Rome sends Ahab
to the fallopian tube

> >o< seraph / * * * stars / ~~~ serpent
> the condensed text

Sly, Silent Shoes

step
into the light, Hansel ... by
sugar ray to the moon

> Lord Slodge
> in his snail-skin coat
> he was quite the thing

they congest the sighway
ghostlings
of spent sperm

> bipolar bears
> with webbed feet ... hopelessly lost
> at the North Hole

in the crack house ...
the elves made us sly, silent shoes
from smoke

> Masonic lodge of the gut ...
> psychic tapeworms
> share everybody's shit

we traverse sloth-cats
the size of hills ...
Earth a vague regret

> a city on the penis
> of the Dionysius whale ...
> ... don't ask

space displaces space ...
beguiled only by what we see
we see nothing

Membrane of Souls

Good King Santa Vlad –
one drop of blood from every child
sustains the year

      octopi mernoids -
      a sky is at the centre
      of the mind

eight a.m. shoatsday ...
Terran minds nulled
by humane frequency

      dregs of tea crowded
      with naiads - through the porthole
      a membrane of souls

surrealonauts
exit the cardboard box ...
a dreary nowhere different

      snowqueen ...
      a fingernail paring
      outlasts her

surrogate ...
beneath the hawthorn
a buried foetus buds

      but empty of song ...
      a bottle full
      of songbird throats

a slice of stale bread
invents the colour grey ...
sleep determines nothing

An Interstice

the government sends
updates … a scab forms
in his mind

       inside the wheredrobe
       … an elsewas-cat
       purring shadows

x-rated vision …
the whore
with a hundred eyes

       a lozenge of frozen light
       burns an interstice …
       strings a then to now

how hides Leviathan?
a boneless flatwhale
that knows only mud

       the giraffe ghouls …
       those wallpaper faces hail
       from the distant stars

crisp with autumn …
the leaf dirigible
crackles through the clouds

       immolate
       in the sanctity engine … nuns
       bleed light for the star run

some like it hot …
the mercury girls
rise above us

The Negative Fog

flash-frozen mermaids ...
prices slashed
in the suffermarket aisles

      hangar 666
      the hearts idling
      in a billion, billion flies

the hedge begets ...
cheeping
of sparrow angels

      the here of there ...
      distance passes
      through the spaceleech

'twould twist your tongue
three micecubes chill
old Vlad's vodka

      electric bayou ...
      the mist guitar
      of Johnny C. Through

scales of light the lamps
of the deep ... by the pinch
of her tail he follows

      frozen match-flames ...
      in the negative fog our
      thoughts become brittle

all heart ...
a fatty skin breaks out all over
the tin man

Land of Don't Know Where

birdsong stilled ...
scent of honeysuckle too subtle
to mask genocide

        never ...
        never had the moths
        a need to name men

we sit astride
the pewter dog ... it's your birthday:
collect a year

        she secures the fog
        with a golden cord ... daylight
        is held from the king

the holes
in her mind ... grandmother knits
a tunnel home

        the very first time
        that things were named ... snake
        is the path it takes

secure in the cockpit
of the plutonium shoe ...
one step beyond

        midday he listens
        to the sun ... the crickets
        talk only of themselves

Land of Don't Know Where
the lightning chair
will take you there

Through Drifting Rooms

waiting for their minds
to enter the ice
... zenguins

      my coat of light
      just the rain
      in the dark

headlamp eyes of owls ...
the mice that sleep in my heart
restless in their dreams

      sunlight ...
      a cat leaves the black of its coat
      at the tree's shadow

grass:
memory, storage capacity, energy,
self-generation

      doors of rain slam shut ...
      I post myself through drifting rooms
      to the lake

in the porch
a spider shapes
perfect silence

      I exhale a hat of fog ...
      the moon is smeared
      in its own light

grit-door opening grain
by grain ... ants navigate
with larvae lantern

Millstone Brooch

foxglove junction
pollen satchels full
the stumble bees

       to never age or die ...
       our vitrified children
       ring with the hail fall

pearl divers ...
the day moon
less

       ovum
       menopausal
       fissionize
       magnetar

sexless yet ...
spermatozoa
in the big she

       glass of brine
       each day in preparation ...
       by millstone brooch to Hades

nightshifts of rust ...
the meteor girls
light up on entry

       just murky water -
       '66 my dream
       of a sea-monkey kingdom

beads spill from the rosary ...
the conjoined owl twins
whoo twice twice

Say Again

anchor-stones tied
to his ankles ... the suicide
broaches depth

> barley-darts caught
> in her fur ... forehead bright
> with the moon

previously lived aeons
as grass ... knotted the world
in its place

> pauper princess
> in her newsprint dress ... his hands
> stained black at her breast

in his own words ...
the ventriloquist's dummy
talks for the hand

> the ship in the bottle
> admires its trophy ...
> a me in the house

white tumour-moon
the tides of our marrow
the shift of our bones

> with a pointed key
> she unlocks the sky -
> deluge of grailstones

say again ...
songs by songbirds made of rain
dash upon my windowpane

A Fancy Word

their marriage either
hot or sharp ... the lava wife
sleeps as glass

        sunlight softens
        the silken city ... the gates linger
        with our hands

winged horses graze
the locust clouds ...
grass is mundane

        pouring the darkness
        out of the moon
        then pouring the moon

its firebox burning minds ...
a dream-engine
approaches the station

        can't tell
        witch from witch?
        call the hexterminators

liberated
from the sheet ...
the stain ascends

        they shatter
        into thrushes ...
        the clay golempigeons

Eskimos
have a fancy word for light
they call it snow

Bloody Nora

cherry blossom petals
nail his shadow down …
miles distant he burns

       pucebirds hymning
       in his head … the Angel
       of the Lord is beige

strapped in the falling piano …
the Down Clowns
thumbed that lift

       Bloody Nora …
       so noisy in her coat
       of black and blue

a moment of snail …
space impales itself with light;
light stands still

       a spider's single stitch …
       you join my shoulder
       to the ceiling

a green jelloid house …
dark tadpoles stir deep
in the birthroom

Fathoms

the circus of Dr Now …
wings of hair
plume the perfect plummet

       the x-ray cows
       go oom …
       sunflower nova

drowned sailors absorbed
by the ice shelf… now
the fathoms fathomable

       that acid tongue …
       sulphuric rains
       reign

an egg with two yolks …
Issa and his shadow
eat their light and dim meals

       does darkness age? …
       faint yet
       the stars in twilight

Soft Om Vortex

one-way ...
the entrance enters the exit
of the cornucopia

      atomic fission ...
      all added fractions less
      amount to more

my black cat Smudge ...
the starless night
brings the cold in on his fur

      Nostradamus pours
      an amber portal ... his chamber pot
      frees the past

a potato with wormy eyes
the earth's iPod ...
ten thousand blight-tunes

      jungle magnolias
      opening all at once
      ... a soft om vortex

Resurrection Window
sunlight throws Christ's face
into the wall

      hydrangeas
      suddenly moonlight ...
      moths linger leprous

Beyond the Happened

sent by white light ...
all you mundane dead
reside in the spam box

      still the fokbombs spore
      their scream-fogs ... hedgehorses neigh
      some myth of man

house with whendows ...
outside nothing was happening
beyond the happened

      the master butcher
      converts a leg of lamb ...
      meat laptops send bloodtext

the Angel of Skin
begins to burn ... a pus waits
for Oppenheimer

      today bluebottle blue
      the excrement throne
      of Beelzebub

penetrating ten thousand years ...
the wreck
of the astral ship

Vhuck9

and flavoured to deter rats ...
live forever
as a bowl of sludge

> she secures the fog
> with a golden cord ... daylight
> is held from the king

barking ...
Laika makes entry
in the earthless mind

> Captain Kronk descends
> the soft grotto ... an
> exhalation of become

a twist of his magic
pepper-mill
her lips get hot

> a glass door clinks shut
> the beekeeper arranges
> his beard of bees

her comb grits its teeth ...
Ophelia's knotted hairs
keep their grip on land

> 666 locust wings
> to make that wedding veil
> ... the groom wore sores

maggot vixens
of Vhuck9 ...
men for breakfast

Sieverts of Thought

snore o forty cuckolds
Ali Baba kisses
the lipdoors open

       hence by steam
       to the crushed
       linen city

shiver, salty seadog!
his mussel soup heaves itself
free of the bowl

       the kapok eaters
       became the inside of teddy bear ...
       come, cuddles

his new gm blood-
stream murdered granddad ... APB
for the walking clot

       post gamma-rot of Oz
       ... an aging Dorothy rules
       Palace Guano

Bayard gallops the silted floor
of the Meuse
Europe infills his hoof prints

       towers of glass rise
       from the sea ...
       a vintage brine

Ouija spells CURIE ...
sieverts of thought
light us up

Mutters a Self

ever the snipped seeder
... dandelion stars
caught in the mog's whiskers

       ink bleeds out ...
       pages grey, the book
       mutters a self

growing, grow-
ing into us ... the swami's
endless fingernails

       termite queen
       majestic in girth she births
       her own slavery

Atlantic notion ...
fashions a makeshift TV
from a jellyfish

       Ben Nevis
       ... catching the cloudcat
       by its foggy tail

door after door
in the hexagonal house -
the long shape of in

Dull Soup

paper-thin Annie Thin
her last boyfriend
was pretty cut up

> eat well thou widower ...
> Lot scrapes a seasoning
> for his dull soup

from between the legs
of Miss Scissors
a snip of a thing

> the man with
> X-ray lungs ...
> took our breath away

the Lazy Witch
of the Ease ... stealthily
the Tin Man cans a snore

> the magician's doorknockers
> nothing
> to see here

his origami combatant
floored with a single
ticket punch

> the stone phallus
> one mile high ... we rest
> in its flaccid shadow

The Finger Bank

Earth's turn as dust -
the dead moon
maintains its grin

       in vinegar seas
       a sour eternity
       for the picklemen

fungous bungalow
another Gretel
subsumed

       seen through obsidian glasses...
       the plasma girl
       mimes a cold shoulder

conjoined fractal codes -
flakes of thought the
snowman's mind

       the finger bank ...
       a chaos auditor
       subtracts another digit

Mockery Skin

dreamtime
astral whales nose through
the earth's core

> she opens a nightjar
> the shooting stars
> plead as they fall

folds a million yen
into origami birds
... Hell bleeds a rainbow

> grey lightning...
> a jellifying voice
> enters the woodsman's mind

the rawlplugs loose
in his shoulder blades ... Mockgabriel
drops a wing

> Jack takes it tuft
> by tuft ... up the giraffe's mane
> to Head-in-the-Clouds

she wears
her Mockery Skin ...
we take it seriously

> between guano and the weight
> of sky ... shifting cities built
> of starlings

Her Deepest Breath

feb 14th 1818 ...
child Edgar's charming
beetle wing necklace

       crumbling cakehouse -
       nutjelly and peabutter
       witchwiches

rope trick ...
caught on a minaret
the magic carpet unravels

       chitin tombstones
       Bluebeard buried those wives
       under his nails

She the gritty pith
of an arbutus fruit ...
O Brightness of Brightness

       her deepest breath ...
       ravens of spaceblack
       forevermore

e. dickinson zero boned
... a narrow fellow parts
the couch-grass

       dating the 60-ft woman
       sex
       was a walk-in

translucent songs
of moonstone blue ...
Sirens siren upside-nine

Ten Gigateslas

cosmic particles
voice their origins ...
stellar lint radio

      with the tired light
      of a standard candle
      Fritz brightens furthest suns

imprisonment
an abstract concept ...
working down the salt minds

      our green future ...
      gm viral cheese
      terraforms the moon

ten gigateslas Earthwards ...
hark the eighteen bells
of the Angelus

      blind slug-evolved
      of the deep Martian grottoes ...
      voyages are always down

new stars the work
of the dead stars ...
universe a coppice

      writ ... a court of
      hippocampus bring the oceans
      to a single spot

Pulling at Our Minds

to the moon!
Monsieur d'Range orchestrates
a bridge of ants

        strange purring star -
        the ship's cat begins
        meowing in tongues

transportable AI
made of nano-tea ...
we consult our cups

        Martian moss-mind ...
        tardigrade priests prophesy
        four-billion-year doze

a sheen
on the moon's brow ... oysters shift
at the seafloor

        starlight holds the key
        ... on the hillside
        a grass door

still pulling at our minds
... the gravitational force
of Pluto

Few Realise

in the vacancy alleged
to be sky ...
a moment named crows

      an elephant in every room ...
      the graphene city
      folds in its case

the solid starlight
of moth's smear ... I shut myself
into the wardrobe

      in her cloak
      of starlings ... lime burns a swathe
      behind her

spirits of canaries
flutter in the mine ...
his lungs inhale souls

      Mineday morning
      they take a step
      into smithereens

few realise the Heavens
in cancer .... Fermi
enters the atom

The Moonbeam Road

wheels of fat
adorn his birthday suit
... tusk tusk King Walrus

     sailed the sea
     in a bucket of sea
     saw the deepest ocean

a squeal splits the moon ...
Grandma Wartkins jumps the sky
in her pigskin shoes

     earwigs behold
     the Lego city ... from Heaven descends
     a cornflake

trod the moonbeam road ...
comets trapped as paisleys
on the gypsy's kerchief

     from the egg-fried rice
     a curling dragon of steam ...
     keep to your course

rocking-horse!
take me forwards and backwards
to here

     now truly selfless ...
     she cut herself looking
     with the shaving mirror

an age ...
the time it takes
for time to take

Eternity is Never Done

he dials "angels"
on the Otherbox ... a goldfish
forms in her bladder

      never saw us coming ...
      a glass car shatters
      the light barrier

a soft invasion ...
the treacle robots
just poured themselves in

      eternity is never done ...
      in her grey mousecoat
      she dusts the moon

polishing the crooked shoe ...
an odour of Stilton
grants three wishes

      mind-snails enter
      by spiral ladder ... something niggles
      the bad conscience

a whale breathes us in ...
night in the sea
is deep

Wheezing an Ecstasy

another ossified cloud
shatters
China Town

      forelocked shut …
      the hundred-headed
      circular horse

wheezing an ecstasy …
the astronauts survey
an angel's flake of dust

      annihilated all that's made …
      they rest
      in existential beige

a soft knock of the hammer?
… inside the apricot
a strange gnarled house

      dropped a knife
      in the Nolichucky …
      the hills limp to a stop

a thousand gardens
hide him … the demolished
porcelain golem

To Lose Oneself

Dr Duzzalot's sharks
spoke sharply ... but blunt
on the subject of death

> snail's frail snotbody
> and only one corridor
> to lose oneself in

disintegrated aeons gone ...
ancestries of grass
recorded us

> litmus ...
> Europa's ocean scarlet
> at the dip of our toes

the blind second-guessers ...
next-ray envisioned
they discern clearly

> womb travellers ...
> nascent fey daughters enrapture
> their to-be-fathers

once on that frictionless
glassy planet
there was no stopping us

> light from the hall ...
> the gap under the door
> is the way to between

blind, blind with angels
... please do not remove
the pins from our eyes

A Silence This Profound

circles within circles
of perfection ... the button
in the poor box

> vocabulary of fire ...
> surprisingly
> a word for ice

unlucky under
the moonbeam ladder ...
his shadow splits at his feet

> barely there
> to the naked eye ... distant stars
> long alive, long dead

with feathered hands
wrings out an ounce
of your mind

> a shaking of light ...
> how many moth's lives
> are you worth?

a princess made
of the finest silk ... oh put her on,
my ugly

> another deceptive tune ...
> the one hundred secret names
> of blackbird

the stringless harp
only a silence this profound
will call them

The Other End

mocks the king's counting house ...
the moon spends itself
then earns itself

       toe-deep in the puddle ...
       the trafficked mermaid
       finds comfort on the street

smelling our skins
with their piked tongues ... skink-maids down
at the husband market

       mouths on her fingers
       mouths on her toes ... the princess rides
       a cockatrice horse

the compassionate, the merciful
... our children
tread out the stars

       your majesty overwhelms ...
       Lord Bluebottle's tower
       of excrement

she opens
the bottle of birdsong ...
we brim with daylight

       on the other end
       of the telephone ... the sky
       bemoans its distance

All The Way Down

the magic rope ...
lowering himself
into a mind

> lost your memory
> in a card game
> go back three spaces

legs of jelly &
sixpence under the pillow ...
the bone fairy

> Forest of Hopelessness ...
> moths burst against us
> in fortunes of silver

"tundra and lightning" ...
the fridge sends
a brief biography

> her newly fried house
> of sausage meat ...
> she slices open the basement

those steam-driven shoes ...
the gnomes shovel coal
apace of each pace

> ears of lead, tongues of tin,
> eyes of pewter ... meet the chimps
> of the future

fly Anxiety Airways
going all the way down
with the blues

The Inevitably Lost

deft the hummingbirds
drank deep from your thoughts
and all you knew

> woolless sheep with
> colostomy bags ... perfect herd
> for the space voyage

freckled curtains for the Fuhrer
shyly
they wait to be parted

> sentient rayguns
> bursting
> with life

no sliced fingers in months ...
a stainless goddess
rattles the cutlery

> Rothko's last painting
> SCARLET THREADWAY THROUGH GREY LIFE
> (kitchen floor)

the hapless contortionist
... falling hands first
through his own pockets

> invisible waiting room
> ... seating for
> the inevitably lost

runny eyelets?
swollen tongues?
you've got the shoe 'flu, son

The Prince Puzzles

she chalked a grave e
on the pavement ... stepping out
in beef wellingtons

       Snot-Eyed Jack ...
       lived in the sinus cavity
       of that giant for years

Three revs of the engine
commands compliance ...
genie in the throttle

       the body stays at home ...
       double-jointed minds   /   soldered to starlight

if we were once star stuff
... let's re-climb the silver ladder
through the sky

       a child's fancy
       riding safe in the ear   /   of the Horsehead Nebula

out of her mind
granny knitted starshoes
then stepped into our hearts

       who was that weird woman?
       the prince puzzles
       over the glass gloves

magic spent matches ...
in their memory of fire
we'll have light again

       fifteen thousand gold chairs
       one on top of the other ...
       Good King Wobble

Another Sheet of Sky

the teapot Djinn …
by her third cup the vicar's wife
finds God

on the octahedral planet …
we grasp new angles   /   of gravity

hot in his circuitry coat
fingers always
on the buttons

not in his right mind
the telepath opens
someone else's eyes

yet another
damp suitor … her heart of coal
still unlit

retro me, Satanas …
crowded with thought the thoughtless
filled that space

the frockodile's wardrobe …
every dress comes   /   with its own teeth

the staircase
hidden in the suitcase … the Devil departs
with my clothes

cried their blue tears
into candle moulds … their sorrow
exhaled as soap

life on scale-model Earth …
we paste another
sheet of sky overhead

Seeming Space

where silence lies heavy ...
blackbird's beak a keepsake
deep in her spacesuit

       some kind of interference
       " ... rodents thread
       my persuade shoes ..."

scab by scab Dr Anjellig
moves Undone Bridge
to Loss Hinges

       in their blue sinstripe suits
       with vulva
       pockets

the snorting meadows ...
tip-toe
through the pigslips

       they'll be forever children
       till their cryosleep
       ends

fill your mind
to ride
the telepathic horse

       after eating the pie chart ...
       silence descends
       over the need for need

in each follicle
billions   /   of souls

the stars so spaced
       seeming
space so dark

One Last Time

he steps upon
the sharpest surface …
this place goes through you

> nothing to hold its tears …
> with a sideways glance
> the winged eyeball departs

solitaire football
… the pitch declares
a foul

> something descends …
> clouds made of silk
> do not bode well

nineteen partings
the wig from Altair 3
had ideas of its own

> o purest white
> the snow whored itself
> over everything

inside the lemon pip …
the bitter empress
seethes yellow

> Sputnik-tinned Laika
> did you bark
> one last time?

The Nothingness Kit

a heart cold from un
-requited passion ... all days
are nights to the sun

they married and lived
in a chestnut ... ate promises
from tins

death an even number ...
moths ambidextrous
in their embrace of flame

      the coal sculpture stallions
      burned for days ...
      we reddened in their beauty

those lips so kissable ...
briars trip
from her tongue

      empty yourselves of hope ...
      the nothingness kit
      comes minus instructions

land mime ...
with a scissors of two fingers
she snips a nowhere

      Dr Dosomething ...
      the bedbugs send representatives
      to the king

These Lies Colour

sun sets in the jar ...
old uncle wasp
took the marmalade lanes

      playing cakes and bladders
      ... the dice
      seem oddly incontinent

mining an ethanol cloud ...
in the vastness of space
we'll still act small

      an equation
      that represents the universe   / is a universe

copyright trespass ...
throughout the labyrinth a
labyrinth of string

      love, Granny Wenceslas ...
      a Christmas jumper made
      of the driven snow

plagiarist bird, six letters
... the crossword puzzle
becomes self-aware

      the sky nudges him
      on the back ... Issa can handle drink;
      but nature?

integrating
with local communities ...
Citizen Ebola

      spectral reflectance
      of a grey moon ...
      we call these lies colour

Ta Da!

a full moon ...
indiscriminate use
of the nuclear family

    Neptune was
    a forgone blue ...
    black is the new black

Picasso discovers
misdirection ... the cubist's nude
spreads her legs

    a winged penis
    not quite the lift
    you'd imagine

nineteen
woodlouse children ...
the classroom under the stone

    after one hundred
    years in concrete ... the frog
    still keeping time

in memoriam
to the meadow ... the solid bronze
meadow

    the telepathic horses ...
    from high boughs the boys
    shake the apples free

and when, your highness,
the stone spaceship is spent ...
ta da! a comet

On the Way to Granny's

a vogue for bespoke candles
… haggles a price
for the giant's earwax

      the hole in his bucket
      a witch's dripping heart
      withers the thistles

shapes of men burnt
into the lawn ... a hanging rope
made from starlight

      the house was built
      from pure sweat ... wiping one's boots
      on a carpet of tongues

each step of the stairs
thick with irises ... granny's grave
in the attic

      your kingdom-in-a-box ...
      naked emperor, enter
      the stark wardrobe

her pearl smile, her bright eye
… a million bumble coats
sewn for her train

A Coat of Brownriver

inside the crocodile ...
the young girl could count seconds
forever

     silken fingered
     the nautilus discerns
     the sea joints

tin mice rewind
at his feet ... Insomnia arrives
by grandfather-clock

     not much left
     after the bombs ... the dust, disturbed,
     holds a conference

ninety-nine milky eyes
only the troll mouse
sees the none others

     the crone and her geese ...
     shadow puppets taunt
     the amputees

the Emperor dressed
as night for the blind
then as naked light

     lest the princess of apple flesh
     would rot ...
     he made a crumble

the milk
of bolted lettuce ... in a coat
of brownriver Alice drowned

Eating Blue

their frolicsome barking
just lights us up ...
the electric seals

> gods have all the time
> for slowness ... yes, the chalk horse
> will drag the hill

I've been walking
around in squares ... this is nothing
but a wrecked angle

> a rather baroque
> brass key ... thirty-six tubas
> open Jericho

everything bad concerning
all the good luck ...
the misfortune cookie

> silent underfoot as moss ...
> those moccasins nevertheless
> spoke well

I see a woman
eating blue from the sky ...
Is there a Richard here?

> your names will be
> inscribed on lettuce ... the snails
> take the salt path

sadly, that marriage
went up the chimney ...
his moth-winged wife

Oh and Oh and Oh

that's Mister Cow Shed
to you ... rivets in the tin roof
pick up Vega

       innocence trumps knowledge
       ... goldfinches flocked
       to the anomalous orb

never neither in nor out
of the wardrobe ...
the never-ending dress

       this deters vampires?
       a pinking shears
       to stop the daylight fraying

the straw best inserted
through the mind ... there's a knack
to sipping souls

       a purple stain broached
       the exosphere ... how regal
       we all now shine

Come, my ladybirds ...
oh and oh and oh,
the queen dressed in aphids!

       hurt umber ...
       that rare pigment
       from the last human whimper

Sir Bland's castle ...
windows of grey gelatine
look out on Sorrowdise

Mother-of-pearl House

the invisible cat
wore the stairs on its back
we'd sleep in its purr

      a thrush's beak, four
      gold clothes-pegs, a wish, a bee's
      buzz ... nanna's purse bursts

mother-of-pearl house
rainbows in every room
plus the ghost of the sea

      child made of steam
      whether he's real or not
      is immaterial

remembered pore by pore
 ... coal-dust invoked the face
of the dead miner

      defining a new dimension
       ... the absence of snail
      in the snail shell

thousandth birthday
his shadow thicker
wherever it rests

      news from the bright knight
      his sunlight sword
      pierces the letterbox

the moat of his castle
solid gold ...
a fabulously drowned Midas

The Lost Things

cuttings
from the root beer ... a stain
spreads through the lawn

> the housefly zizzes ...
> through its windows
> we see the blurrity of life

an expanded childhood ...
teddyphant
filled up my room

> the crunch and jelly of snails
> ... a snakeskin dress
> for Princess Slither

two drops essence of broken heart
one drop vanilla ...
Knave of Ice Cream

> a slice of space
> fell into the Vatican ...
> Heaven is merciless

Zoroaster, tigers, ice
... the lost things
of Earth

> an extraordinary jumper ...
> Gran knitted a room
> then went inside

"... enthnarra logron ..."
the flock wallpaper
picks up a signal

The Dadaist Spaceman

seated in coherent sound
the invasioners
came with a bang

        eaters of steam
        velvet men greet us
        in the clouds of Jupiter

his house of string ...
walls and roof anchored taut
to conflicting gravities

        space-time math in geometric
        volumes ... pine cone languages
        rot down

in the water-spider's
bathysphere ...   /   they take   /   their precarious breaths

        we name our bombs
        without a thought ... without a thought
        we bomb the nameless

the Dadaist spaceman ...
in his onion socks
he purifies the gloom

        grounded in the snow globe
        the sky awaits its return
        to the sky

the hall of moonlight ...
she leaves out a glass of ilk
for the ancestors

Tea Time is O

porcelain rocket ship ...
ladies, prepare to press
the shatter button

        travelled by shuttlecock
        to another Dimension
        ... returned forthwith

horses without skin
gallop their guts loose ...
how pure the burnished sky

        holes in his pockets
        money was nothing
        to the nillionaire

nightshade muffins
tea time is o
ver in no time

        let's eat the navigator ...
        no singing and dancing
        in Angri-La

at the Tree of Knowledge
... there was an old woman
who swallowed a why

        peruse the professor's
        collection of shouts?
        he wouldn't hear of it!

in memory of
our invisible friends ... when childhood died
they died

The Tip of His Tie

space mission … whirligig beetles
dance the stars reflected
on the pond

cheap to run,
you'll hardly feel the motion …
granny's time travel commode

a face for every day …
his heptahedron
marsupial girlfriend

Five Two Two
Unicorn Avenue … the postman
arrives in a wish

even higher, higher, we say …
by stairs carpet
to the glazed moon

the zero-g diet …
lunch
goes floating by

Trump sends forth
the tip of his tie … we're gunna
sartorialize 'em

you drinking
that polonium tea or not?
Death is sick of waiting

There is no, I repeat no
Avian Flu
In Cloud-Cuckoo-Land

Let the Dark

the child draws
an angel ... Heaven is
lopsided and pure

       godfactory product 5 ...
       furry molecules
       of atomic love

tortoise ran
with an idea ... deliver oneself
as a box

       the snake speaks
       in esses ... steam infiltrates
       a dream

the chalk mountains
slowly slowly
draw an ocean

       blackened bodies
       of Hiroshima ... that day the deeps
       of space widened

over the mountains
the flying lantern dims ...
let the dark break our fall

Acknowledgements:

The poems in this collection first appeared in the following journals and anthologies, and grateful acknowledgement and thanks is offered to their numerous editors: *A New Ulster; Bone Orchard Poetry; Bones; The Burning Bush II; The Café Review; CanCan; Carcinogenic; Census 3; Chair Poetry Evenings (India); Circa Review; Danse Macbre; Dead Snakes; Dreams & Nightmares; The 2012 Dwarf Stars Anthology; The Enchanting Verses Literary Journal; Èpico Submundo-literatura & Cultura; Eye to the Telescope; The Galway Review; Grievous Angel; hedgerow; Live Encounters; The Mind[less]Muse; microcosms; Miracle e-zine; The Mystic Nebula; Negative Suck; Notes from the Gean; Otoliths; Outburst Magazine; The Penny Dreadful; Per Diem January 2020 / The Haiku Foundation; poeticdiversity: the litzine of Los Angeles; Prune Juice; Revival; roadrunner; Rose Red Review; The 2012 Rhysling Anthology; Silver Blade; Southword; Stanzas; Twice Upon A Time; Versus Literary Journal; The Weary Blues; World Haiku Review* and *Ygdrasil*.

The individual verse *anorexic girl* received a **Dwarf Stars Nomination** for 2012.

The individual verse *slit sea cucumber* received a **Rhysling Nomination** for 2012.

The sequences, *A State of Mind* and *Beaks of Nowl*, first appeared in Èpico Submundo-literatura & Cultura, April 2011, under the title of *Natural Science, Spiritual Nature* in both English and Portuguese.

The Introduction, originally under the title *Transcending the Mortal Universe: Scifaiku as Compressed Signal*, first appeared as an article in The Weary Blues Volume VI, guest-edited by Cal Doyle.

About the Author

John W. Sexton was born in 1958 and identifies with the Aisling poetic  tradition. His work spans vision poetry, contemporary fabulism and tangential surrealism. He is the author of seven poetry collections, the most recent being: The Offspring of the Moon (Salmon Poetry 2013), Futures Pass (Salmon Poetry 2018), and Visions at Templeglantine (Revival Press 2020). A chapbook of his surrealist poetry, Inverted Night, came out from SurVision in April 2019. His next collection, The World Under the World, is forthcoming from Salmon Poetry. Under the ironic pseudonym of Sex W. Johnston he has recorded an album with legendary Stranglers frontman, Hugh Cornwell, entitled *Sons of Shiva*, which was released on Track Records. He is a past nominee for The Hennessy Literary Award and his poem The Green Owl was awarded the Listowel Poetry Prize 2007 for best single poem. In 2007 he was awarded a Patrick and Katherine Kavanagh Fellowship in Poetry.

Praise for the Author

"John W. Sexton's *The Nothingness Kit* is, in its first and foremost paradox, full of stuff. This collection of 'scifaiku' - haiku which abandon the lapidary strictures with which the form is sometimes burdened to form speculative-fiction narratives - forms a dense forest of wordplay, a pungent pastoral through which figures from myth, folklore and popular culture skip, stumble and thread their way. Sometimes sexy, sometimes scary, silly in its ancient sense of *blessed, touched by the divine*, this is a cosmic ride not to be missed."

- Kit Fryatt; poet and lecturer in English

"It is the job of the poet, above everything, to surprise us, to make new what we once thought of as ordinary, and for the king to be "pleased with his deception". This kingpoet has been pleasantly deceiving us for decades now. As one of Ireland's major, and criminally underrated poets, he has stirred us and whirred our imaginations to all kinds of frenzies, not only in his relentless quest for new forms and delights but in his mesmeric live performances too."

- Colin O'Sullivan, novelist, author of The Starved Lover Sings, The Dark Manual, My Perfect Cousin (all from Betimes Books)

"In The Nothingness Kit, John W. Sexton, 'surrealonaut', daringly untethers haiku in microgravity and lets the form float up against the gamut of his imaginative fancies. The unusual form, hybrid gendai scifaiku, becomes a reservoir for everything from Laika to shoes made of smoke to Johnny Cash to radioactive tea. Spatial and temporal relations blur 'inside the wheredrobe', in 'the house with whendows', and we are in the very bittersweet meltdown of dream."

- Dean Browne, author of Kitchens at Night (smith/doorstop); winner of the Geoffrey Dearmer Prize, 2021